Daily Readings with
Brother Lawrence

Daily Readings with Brother Lawrence

Arranged and introduced by
Robert Llewelyn

Templegate Publishers/Springfield, Illinois

First published in 1985 by
Darton, Longman and Todd Ltd
89 Lillie Road, London SW6 1UD

All royalties earned by the sale
of this book are being given to
The Julian Shrine, c/o All Hallows
Rouen Road, Norwich

First published in the United States in 1986 by
Templegate Publishers
302 E. Adams St./P.O. Box 5152
Springfield, Illinois 62705

ISBN 0-87243-144-4

'We may make an oratory of the heart wherein to retire from time to time to converse with him in humility, meekness and love.' (Brother Lawrence)

Contents

Brother Lawrence:
His Life and Teaching

Artists and craftsmen of whatever skill have this in common: they make what they do look absurdly easy. It is not otherwise with Brother Lawrence, the subject of these pages. His particular art, as described in his own often repeated words, was that of the practice of the presence of God. Some might describe it as the art of prayer, or as the art of living, or perhaps as the art of loving God and his creation. The words chosen are secondary, as too are the descriptions by which the awareness of God's presence, known often only in the obscurity of faith, became the overriding reality of his life. More important is the life itself for, as one who knew him well tells us, his example was a stronger inducement than any arguments he could propose:

His very countenance was edifying; such a sweet and calm devotion appearing in it could not but affect the beholders. And it was observed that in the greatest hurry of business in the kitchen he still preserved his recollection and heavenly-mindedness. He was never hasty nor loitering, but did each thing in its season with an even, uninterrupted composure and tranquillity of spirit. 'The time of business', he said, 'does not differ with me from the time of prayer; and in the noise and clatter of my kitchen, while several persons are at the same time calling for different things, I possess God in as great tranquillity as if I were on my knees at the Blessed Sacrament.'[1]

BROTHER LAWRENCE'S LIFE

Nicolas Herman, known to millions today as Brother Lawrence, was born of humble parentage in Lorraine in eastern France in about the year 1611. After a careful and devout Christian upbringing[2] he joined the army in his late teens. The Thirty Years War with Germany across the border had broken out in his childhood and we may assume he became drawn into it with many young men of his age. At eighteen years he passed through the experience of conversion which he relates in the first of four conversations with the Abbé Joseph de Beaufort, vicar general to Cardinal Noailles. The Abbé was drawn to Brother Lawrence for his simple and unaffected goodness. He later collected some of his letters and maxims

1 This passage is commonly printed with others at the end of the fourth conversation with the comment that they are taken from other sources. The words of Brother Lawrence quoted above come from *Les Moeurs et Entretiens du Frère Laurent* by the Abbé de Beaufort, in the section preceding the *Entretiens* (Conversations); the remainder is based on *L'Eloge du Frère Laurent* by the same author. For reasons of space the passage is not quoted again in this book.
2 The Abbé de Beaufort says that his parents educated him carefully, putting before him the maxims of all the saints and the way of the gospel.

and published them, together with the carefully recorded conversations, in two volumes shortly after Lawrence's death in 1691. The letters and conversations have come down to us today under the general title of *The Practice of the Presence of God*. They have appeared in English in many editions based on a translation made in 1724. The present book, which draws on a translation of 1824, arranges them in a form for daily reading over a period of two months, as in the other books of this series. There is a depth and wisdom in the writings of Brother Lawrence which may easily be missed in the straight reading of his little book.

Brother Lawrence's army service ended abruptly with a Swedish raid on his native village of Rambervilliers in which he was wounded (leaving him permanently lame) and forced to retire.

After a period of convalescence in his parents' home, he entered the employment of William de Fuibert, treasurer to the king of France. Serving as a footman, Lawrence describes himself as 'a great awkward fellow who broke everything' and tells of his desire for the monastic life. His wish was granted when he was admitted to the Carmelite Order in Paris, serving as the monastery cook for thirty years and, for a time, as cobbler. In spite of the quiet and unobtrusive manner of his life he acquired considerable fame in his later years and Parisians from all sections of society, sensing his innate goodness and holiness, were eager to share his company and learn from him.

A REALISTIC APPRAISAL

It is possible to have a romantic and unrealistic conception of Brother Lawrence as we picture him, perhaps, working peacefully year after year at a task congenial to him in the quiet and idyllic surroundings of a monastery kitchen. In such circumstances it ought not to be too difficult to preserve equanimity of mind and to live consciously in the knowledge and presence of God. With no telephone to contend with, no callers, no children needing attention, none of the many distractions the modern housewife may expect, it is hardly surprising that such an exalted way of life was possible. The book corrects this mistaken view. We learn, for example, that he had a strong natural aversion to cooking, and the opening page of the text suggests that work in the garden amidst the beauties of nature may have been his natural love. Perhaps his lameness made this impossible, though it must often too have presented a problem in the kitchen. As for the quiet and calm of his surroundings we have already read of the hurry and bustle of the kitchen with all around clamouring for their needs. Monastic cooks do in fact have to work under peculiarly demanding conditions. Apart from the task of cooking for numbers and commonly with a minimum of suitable equipment, meals have to be supplied precisely on time with the cooks often enough having to spend the final quarter of an hour singing an Office in the community chapel. Little wonder if the housewife's task is sometimes the envy of the monk or nun!

A superficial acquaintance with this brief spiritual classic may well leave another false impression: that Brother Lawrence's serene and joyous life came almost naturally to him, being in some measure at least the overflow of a cheerful and buoyant temperament. A careful reading will not support that view and reference to the writings of the Abbé de Beaufort confirms and enlarges what is only touched on in these pages. There is a good deal to suggest that in the order of nature Brother Lawrence had an anxious if not melancholic disposition. Writing within a year or two of his death the Abbé tells of the doubts he experienced at one time of his final salvation, sufferings which Brother Lawrence could only liken to the pains of hell. In this state he would leave his place of work to seek out a solitary place where was to be found a representation of Christ tied to the pillar. In an abundance of tears he would pour out his heart to God, entreating him not to allow him to perish since he trusted him wholly and had no intention other than to please him.

Yet his pains were not eased. In his sought-out solitude, where he had hoped (in the vivid imagery of the Abbé's words) to find a safe haven, he found only heavy seas churned by raging tempests. His spirit was disturbed even as a vessel battered by winds and storm, abandoned by its pilot, and he knew not what course to take. Yet more, his soul was plunged into such despondency and thick darkness that he could receive help neither from heaven nor earth.

THE CONFLICT RESOLVED

It is interesting to learn how Brother Lawrence's conflict was relieved. At this stage we might expect to hear that he made an act of faith in Christ for his salvation and that, as with Bunyan's Christian at the foot of the cross, the burden of sin fell from his back. But that was not yet to be and at the time of which we are here speaking the conflict was resolved in a different way. At this time when the haunting memory of his sins was upon him[1] it was only, he tells us, when he had reconciled himself to live out all his days in trouble and disquiet – 'which did not at all diminish the trust I had in God, and which served only to increase my faith'[2] – that he found himself suddenly changed, experiencing a profound inward peace, his soul finding in God its centre and place of rest. Thus, instead of running away from the suffering of a troubled mind, he accepted it and was content to live with it for as long as might be, putting all his confidence in God whose strength would be made perfect in his weakness. So it was, with constant renewals and turnings again after failure, that his life came to be marked with an aura of peace and joy. Many will find consolation and strength from Brother Lawrence's experience at this point.

1 This is not, of course, to make Brother Lawrence 'the greatest of all sinners', excepting in the sense that that is true of us all. His was rather the insight of the saints – *he saw it to be so*.
2 p. 66

LOVE, THE DOMINANT FEATURE

It is love which is the dominant feature of these pages. Adapting, in the years following his conversion, the worldling's 'eat, drink and be merry, for tomorrow we die' to its counterpart on the plane of heroic sanctity, he reasoned quaintly with himself that although he might be denied the joy and privilege of loving God through all eternity, at least nothing could or would deprive him of practising his love in this life.[1] Christian love is expressed in the exercise and direction of the will, often, it may be, reinforced by pleasurable affections and feelings. But it is not dependent upon these, and indeed it is expressed not infrequently when the emotional side of our nature is for the time being dried up or, yet more, it may be acting against us. One way in which Brother Lawrence expressed his love for God was in the constancy of his prayer-life – what he calls his conversation with God or his practice of God's presence – but there must have been many occasions when his emotions, given free rein, would have taken him (humanly speaking) to a more pleasurable task. The deceptive simplicity of Brother Lawrence's way may make us think for a moment that here we have a religion without tears. To take, however, any one of many passages from the pages which follow, and to

1 So, too, at one stage St Francis de Sales, whom de Caussade quotes with approval. The Church's view may be found in Gordon Wakefield's article 'Disinterested Love' in *A Dictionary of Christian Spirituality*. SCM Press 1983.

endeavour to practise its message for but the brief period of a single morning, will assure us that this is far from being so. 'There is need of fidelity', he writes, 'in those times of dryness, or insensibility and irksomeness in prayer, by which God tries our love for him.'[1]

Brother Lawrence's life was not exciting as the world would understand it, but it was marked by the quiet heroism which lifted every action into the light of God's presence, making it a sacrificial offering for the love of God. 'Our sanctification', he tells us, 'does not depend on our changing our works, but in doing for God's sake that which commonly we do for our own'[2] and again, 'We ought not to be weary of doing little things for the love of God who regards, not the greatness of the work, but the love with which it is performed.'[3] Whether he was engaged in the humdrum task of cooking in the monastery, or on an expedition to buy provisions for the brethren, or simply picking up a straw from the ground, his action was directed, as far as in him lay, to the honour and glory of God. This last simple task provides a favourite illustration used three times within the scope of this book. 'He was pleased when he could take up a straw from the ground for the love of God, seeking him only, and nothing else, not even his gifts.'[4] As Julian of Norwich found God's love for all creation symbolized in his care for a hazelnut in the palm of her hand, so to raise a straw from the ground

1 p. 25   2 p. 43   3 p. 45   4 p. 27

solely for the love of God focused for Brother Lawrence the love which must quicken and inform every activity.

COMPLEMENTARY WAYS OF PRAYER

Brother Lawrence's method of prayer may be seen as complementary to one which many find helpful today: frequent repetition of some familiar form of words, such as the Jesus Prayer associated particularly with the Orthodox Church. This is an authentic and well-tried way and is well suited to the prayer-life of many people. For others it can become unduly mechanical and thus unreal. For them the way of Brother Lawrence may make possible a deeper freshness and spontaneity. Yet, however much we are helped by one method or another, we must constantly return to the basic and over-riding truth that only the Holy Spirit can teach us how to pray. Prayer is better seen, not as something which we do, but as something which, through grace received, the Holy Spirit is enabled to do within us. In repetitive prayer, for example, it is better if we can see the words working upon us (or, more precisely, the Holy Spirit through the words) rather than seeing ourselves as working upon them. This will develop our awareness of God's action, an awareness which for some may be more easily realized through the way which Brother Lawrence commends. His way, we may remark, is, as we would expect, the closer of the two to the genius of French spirituality as exemplified by François de Sales, Jean-Pierre de Caussade, Fénelon[1] and others. Everyone must, however, discover what is best for themselves, and for many the two ways may present themselves not as alternatives but as supplementing and complementing one another.

How, then, may we describe his way? For the most part it will be made clear through the pages of this book. Here we may briefly depict it as a way in which we are to see all our actions as moments of communion with God. Our communion is to be preserved and deepened by frequent pauses in which we may hold short converse with him. This will not take any set form – it may be simply the elevation of the heart – and if we use words, they will flow spontaneously and gladly from the simplicity of our hearts. Especially will this loving converse take place in times of temptation or distress, or when our hearts are dry or after we have fallen away from God. It must often be that faith alone is our support; indeed the pre-eminence of love must not blind us to the pre-cedence of faith. 'God has many ways of drawing us to himself. He sometimes hides himself from us; but faith alone, which will not fail us in time of need, ought to be our support, and the foundation of our confidence,

1 Fénelon held Brother Lawrence and his teaching in high esteem. He once visited him in sickness, and in a letter to the Comtesse de Montboron tells her that though he was very ill he was very happy (*gai*). He wrote, '*Le Frère Laurent est grossier* (rough? uncouth?) *par nature et délicat* (refined or sensitive) *par grâce*', adding that this was a pleasing combination which manifested God in him.

which must be all in God.'[1] At all times we are to endeavour to act recollectedly and not allow our minds to stray too far. We are to attend to our tasks quietly and lovingly asking God to accept our work. In such a way our motives will be purified and we shall be purged of the destructive effects of self-love.

BROTHER LAWRENCE'S PRAYER-LIFE

To Brother Lawrence himself was given a high degree of mystical prayer. His most revealing letter was written to a priest-religious to whom he desires to give some description of his state. Together with some of his other letters it is undated, but the internal evidence indicates that it was written in the same period as the dated letters, that is to say, in the last ten years of his life. This is the period when the Quietist controversy was exercising the mind of the Church, and three years before Brother Lawrence's death Madame Guyon[2] had suffered her first imprisonment. It is not surprising that in the feverish mood of the time Brother Lawrence's way had by some been called

1 p. 85
2 One wishes that Madame Guyon could have been allowed to continue her passive ways in peace. In the event her persecution in some degree backfired in that it drew from her such patience, charity and fortitude as did much to testify to the authenticity of her way of prayer for herself. In its condemnation the Church will have had chiefly in mind the safeguarding of the body of the faithful. Ronald Knox once remarked (and it was more than a clever quip) that the trouble with the Quietists was that they would not keep quiet!

into question and, in the letter to which we are referring, he finds it necessary to defend himself against delusion. This need not detain us here: more important is the account Brother Lawrence gives of his own experience in the spiritual life:

> I have quitted all forms of devotion and set prayers but those to which my state obliges me. And I make it my only business to persevere in his holy presence, wherein I keep myself by a simple attention and an absorbing passionate regard to God, which I may call an actual presence of God; or, to speak better, a silent and secret conversation of the soul with God, which often causes in me joys and raptures inwardly, and sometimes also outwardly, so great that I am forced to use means to moderate them and to prevent their appearance to others . . . My most usual method is this simple attention, and such a general passionate regard to God, to whom I find myself often attached with greater sweetness and delight than that of an infant at the mother's breast; so that if I dare use the expression, I should choose to call this state 'the breasts of God', for the inexpressible sweetness which I taste and experience there.[1]

THE CLOSING DAYS

'I hope from his mercy the favour of seeing him in a few days.'[2] They were almost the closing

1 pp. 67, 68
2 p. 90

words of his last letter written on Tuesday, 6 February 1691. On Thursday (the Abbé tells us) he took to his bed, suffering greatly. Out of his pain he tells his brothers that his spirit is happy and content. On Sunday 11 February he received the last sacraments in the presence of the community. On being asked how he was occupied as death approached, he replied: 'I am doing what I shall do through all eternity – I bless God, I praise God, I adore him and love him with all my heart. It is our one occupation, my brothers, to worship him and love him without concern for anything else.'

A brother asked him if he would entreat God that he might be given the true spirit of prayer. Brother Lawrence told him that he, too, must play his part if he were to be worthy of such a gift. They were his last words, and at nine o'clock on the following morning, Monday 12 February, in full possession of his faculties, without pain or struggle, he 'gave back his soul to God in the peace and calm of one who falls asleep'.

Robert Llewelyn
The Julian Shrine
c/o All Hallows
Rouen Road
Norwich

The

indling
Of Love

The Kindling of Love

The first time I saw Brother Lawrence was on 3 August 1666. He told me that God had done him a singular favour, in his conversion at the age of eighteen. He said that:

One winter day, seeing a tree stripped of its leaves, and considering that within a little time the leaves would be renewed, and after that the flowers and fruit appear, he received a high view of the providence and power of God, which has never since been effaced from his soul.

This view had perfectly set him loose from the world, and kindled in him such a love for God that he could not tell whether it had increased during the more than forty years that he had lived since.

He said that he had been footman to M. Fuibert, the treasurer, and that he was a great awkward fellow who broke everything.

He had desired to be received into a monastery, thinking that he would there be made to smart for his awkwardness and the faults he should commit, and so he should sacrifice to God his life with its pleasures; but God had disappointed him, he having met with nothing but satisfaction in that state.

A Sense of God's Presence

Brother Lawrence said:

That we should establish in ourselves a sense of God's presence by continually conversing with him.

It was a shameful thing to quit his conversation to think of trifles and fooleries.

We should feed and nourish our souls with high notions of God, which would yield us great joy in being devoted to him.

We ought to quicken or enliven our faith. It was lamentable that we had so little; and that instead of taking faith for the rule of their conduct, men amused themselves with trivial devotions which changed daily.

The way of faith is the spirit of the Church, and is sufficient to bring us to a high degree of perfection.

Wholly Given to God

Brother Lawrence said:

That we ought to give ourselves up entirely to God, with regard both to things temporal and spiritual.

We should seek our satisfaction only in the fulfilling of God's will, whether he lead us by suffering or consolation.

All would be equal to a soul truly resigned.

There is need of fidelity in those times of dryness, or insensibility and irksomeness in prayer, by which God tries our love for him.

He said that *then* was the time for us to make good and effectual acts of resignation, whereof one alone would often very much promote our spiritual advancement.

Watchfulness Over the Passions

Brother Lawrence said:

That as for the miseries and sins he heard of daily in the world, he was so far from wondering at them that, on the contrary, he was surprised that there were not more, considering the malice that sinners were capable of.

For his part, he prayed for them; but knowing that God could remedy the mischiefs they did, when he pleased, he gave himself no further trouble.

To arrive at such resignation as God requires, we should watch attentively over all the passions which mingle as well in spiritual things as those of a grosser nature.

God would give light concerning those passions to those who truly desire to serve him.

Brother Lawrence went on to say that if it was my desire sincerely to serve God, I might visit him as often as I pleased, without any fear of being troublesome; but if not, that I ought no more to visit him.

Seeking God Only

My second conversation with Brother Lawrence took place on 28 September 1666. In the course of our talk he said:

That !He had always been governed by love, without selfish views, and without concerning himself whether he would be lost or saved; and that having resolved to make the love of God the *end* of all his actions, he had good reason to be well satisfied with his method.

He was pleased when he could take up a straw from the ground for the love of God, seeking him only, and nothing else, not even his gifts.

In order to form a habit of conversing with God continually, and referring all we do to him, we must first apply to him with some diligence.

After a little care we should find his love inwardly excite us to it without any difficulty.

The Night of Purification

Brother Lawrence said:

That he had been long troubled in mind from a sure belief that he was lost; that all the men in the world could not have persuaded him to the contrary; but that he had thus reasoned with himself about it:

'I engaged in a religious life only for the love of God, and I have endeavoured to act only for him: whatever becomes of me, whether I be lost or saved I will always continue to act purely for the love of God. I shall have this good at least, that till death I shall have done all that is in me to love him.'

This trouble of mind had lasted four years, during which he had suffered much; but that since he had ceased to concern himself about heaven or hell, he had passed his life in perfect liberty and continual joy.

He had placed his sins between him and God, as it were to tell him that he did not deserve his favours, but that God still continued to bestow them in abundance.

Our Sufficiency is of God

Brother Lawrence said:

That he expected, after the pleasant days God had given him, he would have his turn of pain and suffering.

He was not uneasy about it, knowing very well that as he could do nothing of himself, God would not fail to give him the strength to bear it.

When an occasion of practising some virtue offered, he addressed himself to God, saying, 'Lord, I cannot do this unless you enable me'; he then received strength more than sufficient.

When he had failed in his duty, he simply confessed his fault, saying to God, 'I shall never do otherwise if you leave me to myself; it is you who must hinder my falling and mend what is amiss.'

After this he gave himself no further uneasiness about it.

Grace to Meet Every Need

Brother Lawrence said:

That we ought to act with God in the greatest simplicity, speaking to him frankly and plainly, and imploring his assistance in our affairs just as they happen. God never failed to grant it, as he had often experienced.

He had been lately sent into Burgundy to buy the provision of wine for the Society, which was a very unwelcome task to him, because he had no turn for business, and because he was lame and could not go about the boat except by rolling himself over the casks.

However, he gave himself no uneasiness about it, nor about the purchase of the wine.

He said to God that it was his business he was about, and that afterwards he found it very well performed.

He had been sent into Auvergne the year before upon the same account; that he could not tell how the matter passed, but that it proved very well.

So, likewise, in his business in the kitchen (to which he had naturally a great aversion) having accustomed himself to do everything there for the love of God, and with prayer, upon all occasions, for his grace to do his work well, he had found everything easy during the fifteen years he had been employed there.

Prayer Carried in the Heart

Brother Lawrence said:

That he was then happily employed in the cobbler's workshop; but that he was as ready to quit that post as the former, since he was always finding pleasure in every condition by doing little things for the love of God.

With him the *set* times of prayer were not different from other times.

He retired to pray, according to the direction of his Superior, but he did not want such retirement or ask for it, because his greatest business did not divert him from God.

As he knew his obligation to love God in all things, and as he endeavoured so to do, he had no need of a director to advise him, but he needed much a confessor to absolve him.

He was very sensible of his faults, but not discouraged by them.

He confessed them to God, but did not plead against him to excuse them.

When he had done so, he peaceably resumed his usual practice of love and adoration.

Useless Thoughts Spoil All

Brother Lawrence said:

That in his trouble of mind he had consulted no one, but knowing only by the light of faith that God was present, he contented himself with directing all his actions to him, doing them with a desire to please him, come what may.

That useless thoughts spoil all.

The mischief began there, but we ought to reject them as soon as we perceived their impertinence to the matter in hand or to our salvation, and return to our communion with God.

At the beginning he had often passed his time appointed for prayer in rejecting wandering thoughts and falling back into them.

He could never regulate his devotion by certain methods as some do. Nevertheless, at first he had meditated for some time, but afterwards that went off in a manner he could give no account of.

Mortification Barren Without Love

Brother Lawrence said:

That all mortifications and other exercises were only useful in so far as they advanced union with God by love.

He had well considered this, and found it the shortest way to go straight to him by a continual practice of love and doing all things for his sake.

All possible kinds of mortification, if they were devoid of the love of God, could not efface a single sin.

We ought without anxiety to expect the pardon of our sins from the blood of Jesus Christ, labouring simply to love him with all our hearts.

God seemed to have granted the greatest favours to the greatest sinners, as more signal monuments of his mercy.

He thought neither of death nor of his sins, nor heaven nor hell, but of doing little things – being incapable of big ones – for the love of God. He had no need to trouble himself further, for whatever followed would be pleasing to God.

Desiring One Thing Only

Brother Lawrence said:

That we ought to make a great difference between the acts of the understanding and those of the will.

The first were comparatively of little value, and the others, all.

Our only business was to love and delight ourselves in God.

The greatest pains or pleasures of this world were not to be compared with what he had experienced of both kinds in a spiritual state.

Hence he was careful for nothing and feared nothing, desiring of God only that he might not offend him.

He had no qualms; for, said he, when I fail in my duty, I readily acknowledge it, saying, 'I am used to doing so; I shall never do otherwise if I am left to myself.'

If he did not fail, then he gave God thanks, acknowledging that the strength came from him.

The
Foundation
Of The
Spiritual
Life

The Foundation of the Spiritual Life

Our third conversation took place on 22 November 1666. Brother Lawrence then told me:

That the foundation of the spiritual life in him had been a high notion and esteem of God in faith; which when he had once well conceived, he had no other care but faithfully to reject at once every other thought, that he might perform all his actions for the love of God.

When sometimes he had not thought of God for a good while, he did not disquiet himself for it.

After having acknowledged his wretchedness to God, he returned to him with so much the greater trust in him as he had found himself wretched through forgetting him.

The trust we put in God honours him much and draws down great graces.

Casting Our Care Upon God

Brother Lawrence said:

That it was impossible not only that God should deceive, but also that he should long let a soul suffer which is perfectly surrendered to him, and resolved to endure everything for his sake.

He had so often experienced the ready succour of divine grace upon all occasions, that from the same experience, when he had business to do, he did not think of it beforehand.

When it was time to do it he found in God, as in a clear mirror, all that it was fit for him to do.

Of late he had acted thus without anticipating care; but before the experience above mentioned, he had been full of care and anxiety in his affairs.

Living in God's Presence

Brother Lawrence said:

That he had no recollection of what things he had done, once they were past, and hardly realized them when he was about them.

On leaving the table he did not know what he had been eating.

With one single end in view, he did all for the love of God, rendering him thanks for that he had directed these acts, and an infinity of others throughout his life.

He did all very simply, in a manner which kept him ever steadfastly in the loving presence of God.

When outward business diverted him a little from the thought of God, a fresh remembrance coming from God invested his soul, and so inflamed and transported him that sometimes he cried out and leaped about and danced like a lunatic.

Abandonment to God: The Sure Way

Brother Lawrence said:

That he was more united to God in his ordinary occupations than when he left them for devotion in retirement, from which he knew himself to issue with much dryness of spirit.

He expected hereafter some great pain of body or mind. The worst that could happen to him would be to lose that sense of God which he had enjoyed so long.

But the goodness of God assured him that he would not forsake him utterly, and that he would give him strength to bear whatever evil he permitted to happen to him.

He therefore feared nothing and had no occasion to consult with anyone, about his soul. That when he had attempted to do it, he had always come away more perplexed, and that as he was conscious of his readiness to lay down his life and be lost for the love of God, he had no apprehension of danger.

Perfect abandonment to God was the sure way to heaven, a way on which we have always sufficient light for our conduct.

A Resolute Heart

Brother Lawrence said:

That in the beginning of the spiritual life we ought to be faithful in doing our duty and denying ourselves; but after that, unspeakable pleasures followed.

In difficulties we need only to have recourse to Jesus Christ and beg his grace; with that everything became easy.

Many do not advance in the Christian way because they stick in penances and particular exercises, while they neglect the love of God, which is the end.

This appeared plainly by their works, and was the reason why we see so little solid virtue.

There was need neither for art nor learning for going to God, but only a heart resolutely determined to apply itself to nothing but him, or for his sake, and to love him only.

Living in God's Presence

My fourth conversation with Brother Lawrence was on 25 November 1667. He discoursed with me very fervently and with great openness of heart, whereof some part is related already.

He told me that all consists in one hearty renunciation of everything which does not lead us to God in order that we may accustom ourselves to a continual conversation with him, with freedom and in simplicity.

We need only to recognize God intimately present with us, and to address ourselves to him every moment.

Thus we may beg his assistance for knowing his will in things doubtful, and for rightly performing those which we plainly see he requires of us; offering them to him before we do them, and giving him thanks when we have done.

In this conversation with God we are also employed in praising, adoring, and loving him unceasingly, for his infinite goodness and perfection.

Doing All for God's Sake

Brother Lawrence said:

That without being discouraged on account of our sins, we should pray for God's grace with perfect confidence, relying on the infinite merits of our Lord Jesus Christ.

God never failed to offer us his grace at every action; he himself distinctly perceived it, and never failed of it, unless when his thoughts had wandered from a sense of God's presence, or he had forgotten to ask his assistance.

God always gives us light in our doubts when we have no other design but to please him, and to act for his love.

Our sanctification does not depend on our changing our works, but in doing that for God's sake which commonly we do for our own.

It was lamentable to see how many people mistook the means for the end, addicting themselves to certain works, which they performed very imperfectly, by reason of their human or selfish regard.

Action, a Way of Prayer

Brother Lawrence said:

That the most excellent method he had found of going to God was that of doing our common business (for him received under obedience) without any view of pleasing men, and (as far as possible) purely for the love of God.

It was a great delusion to think that the times of prayer ought to differ from other times.

We are as strictly obliged to adhere to God by action in the time of action as by prayer in the season of prayer.

His view of prayer was nothing else but a sense of the presence of God, his soul being at that time insensible to everything but divine love.

When the appointed times of prayer were past, he found no difference because he still continued with God, praising him and blessing him with all his might, so that he passed his life in continual joy.

Even so, he hoped that God would give him something to suffer when he should have grown stronger.

God Looks Upon the Love
Behind the Work

Brother Lawrence said:

That we ought, once and for all, heartily to put our whole trust in God, and make a full surrender of ourselves to him, secure that he would not deceive us.

We ought not to be weary of doing little things for the love of God, who regards not the greatness of the work, but the love with which it is performed.

We should not wonder if, in the beginning, we often failed in our endeavours, but that at last we should gain a habit, which will naturally produce its acts in us, without our care, and to our exceeding great delight.

The whole substance of religion was faith, hope and love, by the practice of which we become united to the will of God.

All besides is indifferent, and to be used only as a means that we may arrive at our end, and be swallowed up therein by faith and love.

Love Renders Our Task Easy

Brother Lawrence said:

That all things are possible to him who believes.

They are less difficult to him who hopes.

They are more easy to him who loves, and still more easy to him who perseveres in the practice of these three virtues.

The end we ought to propose to ourselves is to become, in this life, the most perfect worshippers of God we can possibly be, as we hope to be through all eternity.

The greater perfection a soul aspires after, the more dependent it is upon divine grace.

Patience in Troubles

Brother Lawrence said:

That when we enter upon the spiritual life, we should consider and examine to the depths what we are.

We would then find ourselves worthy of all contempt, and not deserving indeed the name of Christians; subject to all kinds of misery and numberless accidents, which trouble us and cause perpetual vicissitudes in our health, in our humour, in our internal and external dispositions; in short, persons whom God would humble by many pains and labours, within as well as without.

After this we should not wonder that troubles, temptations, oppositions and contradictions happen to us from men.

We ought, on the contrary, to submit ourselves to them, and bear them as long as God pleases, as things highly beneficial to us.

An Habitual Sense of God

Being questioned by one of his own Society (to whom he was obliged to open himself) by what means he had attained such an habitual sense of God, Brother Lawrence told him that, since his first coming to the monastery, he had considered God as the end of all his thoughts and desires, as the mark towards which they should tend, and in which they should terminate.

In the beginning of his novitiate he spent the hours appointed for private prayer in thinking of God, so as to convince his mind of, and to impress deeply upon his heart, the divine existence, rather by devout sentiments, and submission to the lights of the Faith, than by studied reasonings and elaborate meditations.

By this short and sure method he exercised himself in the knowledge and love of God, resolving to use his utmost endeavour to live in a continual sense of his presence, and, if possible, never to forget him more.

On
Going
To Work

On Going to Work

Brother Lawrence said:

That when he had thus in prayer filled his mind with great sentiments of that Infinite Being, he went to his work appointed in the kitchen (for he was cook to the Society). There having considered severally the things his office required, and when and how each thing was to be done, he spent all the intervals of his time, as well before as after his work, in prayer.

When he began his business, he said to God, with a filial trust in him: 'O my God, since you are with me, and I must now, in obedience to your commands, apply my mind to these outward things, I beseech you to grant me the grace to continue in your presence: and to this end I ask you to prosper me with your assistance and to receive all my work, and possess all my affections.'

We Can Do Little Things for God

Brother Lawrence said:

'We can do little things for God. I turn the cake that is frying in the pan for love of him, and that done, if there is nothing else to call me, I prostrate myself in worship before him, who has given me grace to work; afterwards I rise happier than a king. It is enough for me to pick up but a straw from the ground for the love of God.'

As he proceeded with his work he continued his familiar conversation with his Maker, imploring his grace and offering to him all his actions.

When he had finished he examined himself how he had discharged his duty; if he had done well, he returned thanks to God; if otherwise, he asked pardon; and without being discouraged, he set his mind right again, and continued his exercise of the presence of God, as if he had never deviated from it.

'Thus,' said he, 'by rising after my falls, and by frequently renewed acts of faith and love, I am come to a state wherein it would be as difficult for me not to think of God as it was at first to accustom myself to it.'

The Practice of the Presence of God

Brother Lawrence wrote:

I have taken this opportunity to communicate to you the thoughts of one of our Society, concerning the wonderful effect and continual succour which he receives from the presence of God. Let you and me both profit by them.

You must know that during the forty years and more he has spent in religion, his continual care has been to be always with God and to do nothing, say nothing, and think nothing that may displease him, and this without any other view than purely for the love of him, and because he (God) deserves infinitely more.

He is now so accustomed to that divine presence that he receives from it continual succour upon all occasions. For above thirty years his soul has been filled with joys so continual, and sometimes so transcendent that he is forced to use means to moderate them, and to prevent their appearing outwardly.

Re-collection When the Mind has Strayed

Brother Lawrence continued:

If sometimes he is a little too much absent from the divine presence, which happens often when he is most engaged in his outward business, God presently makes himself felt in his soul to recall him. He answers with exact fidelity to these inward drawings, either by an elevation of the heart towards God or by a meek and loving regard to him or by such words as love forms on these occasions, as for instance, 'My Lord, behold me, wholly yours: Lord, make me according to your heart.'

And then it seems to him (as in effect he feels it) that this God of love, satisfied with such few words, reposes again, and rests in the depths and centre of his soul.

The experience of these things gives him such an assurance that God is always deep within his soul, that no doubt of it can arise, whatever may betide.

Judge from this what contentment and satisfaction he enjoys, feeling continually within him so great a treasure. No longer is he in anxious search after it, but he has it open before him, free to take of it what he pleases.

Let Us Enter Into Ourselves

Brother Lawrence continued:

This brother complains much of our blindness, and exclaims often that we are to be pitied who content ourselves with so little.

'God's treasure', he says, 'is like an infinite ocean, yet a little wave of feeling, passing with the moment, contents us. Blind as we are, we hinder God and stop the current of his graces. But when he finds a soul permeated with a living faith, he pours into it his graces and favours plenteously; into the soul they flow like a torrent which, after being forcibly stopped against its ordinary course, when it has found a passage, spreads with impetuosity its pent-up flood.'

Yes, we often stop this torrent by the little value we set upon it. But let us stop it no longer. Let us enter into ourselves and break down the barrier which holds us back.

Let us make the most of the day of grace; let us redeem the time that is lost, for perhaps we have but little left.

Death follows us close; let us be well prepared for it; for we die but once, and a miscarriage then is irretrievable.

Not to Advance is to Go Back

Brother Lawrence continued:

I say again, let us enter into ourselves. Time presses, there is no room for delay; each must answer for himself. You, I believe, have taken such effectual measures that you will not be surprised. I commend you for it; it is the one thing needful.

We must, nevertheless, always work at it, for, in the spiritual life, not to advance is to go back.

But those whose spirits are stirred by the breath of the Holy Spirit go forward even in sleep.

If the vessel of our soul is still tossed with winds and storms, let us awake the Lord, who reposes in it, and he will quickly calm the sea.

I have taken the liberty to impart to you these good thoughts, that you may compare them with your own. It will serve again to rekindle and inflame them, if by misfortune (which God forbid, for it would be indeed a great misfortune) they should be, though never so little, cooled.

Let us then both recall our early fervour . . . I will pray for you; do you pray instantly for me.

The Motive is Love

Brother Lawrence wrote:

I have received today two books and a letter from Sister — , who is preparing to make her profession, and upon that account desires the prayers of your holy community, and yours in particular. . . I will send you one of these books which treat of the presence of God, a subject which, in my opinion, contains the whole spiritual life: and it seems to me that whoever duly practises it will soon become spiritual.

I know that for the right practice of it the heart must be empty of all else, because God wills to possess the heart alone; and as he cannot possess it alone unless it be empty of all besides, so he cannot work in it what he would unless it be left vacant to him.

There is not in the world a kind of life more sweet and delightful than that of a continual walk with God.

Those only can comprehend it who practise and experience it; yet I do not advise you to do it from that motive.

It is not pleasure which we ought to seek in this exercise; but let us do it from the motive of love, and because God would have us so walk.

All the World May Do It

Brother Lawrence continued:

Were I a preacher, I would, above all other things, preach the practice of the presence of God; and were I a director, I would advise all the world to do it, so necessary do I think it, and so easy, too.

Ah! knew we but the need we have of the grace and assistance of God, we would never lose sight of him – no, not for a moment.

Believe me: this very instant make a holy and firm resolution nevermore wilfully to stray from him, and to live the rest of your days in his sacred presence, for love of him surrendering, if he think fit, all other pleasures.

Set heartily about this work, and if you perform it as you ought, be assured that you will soon find the effects of it.

I will assist you with my prayers, poor as they are. I commend myself earnestly to yours and those of your holy community, being theirs, and more particularly Yours, — .

The Still Point at the Centre

Brother Lawrence wrote:

I wonder that you have not given me your thoughts on the little book I sent to you, and which you must have received. Pray, set heartily about the practice of it in your old age; it is better late than never.

I cannot imagine how religious persons can live satisfied without the practice of the presence of God. For my part, I keep myself retired with him in the very centre of my soul as much as I can, and while I am with him I fear nothing, but the least turning away from him is to me insupportable.

This exercise does not much fatigue the body; yet it is proper to deprive it sometimes, nay often, of many little pleasures which are innocent and lawful, for God will not permit that a soul which desires to be devoted entirely to him should take other pleasures than with him: that is more than reasonable.

I do not say that therefore we must put any violent constraint on ourselves. No, we must serve God in a holy freedom; we must do our business faithfully, without trouble or disquiet, recalling our mind to God meekly, and with tranquillity, as often as we find it wandering from him.

The Means Subordinate to the End

Brother Lawrence continued:

It is, however, necessary to put our whole trust in God, laying aside all other cares, and even some particular forms of devotion, though very good in themselves, yet such as one often engages in unreasonably, because these devotions are only means to attain the end.

So when by this practice of the presence of God we are with him who is our end, it is then useless to return to the means.

Then it is that abiding in his holy presence, we may continue our commerce of love, now by an act of adoration, of praise, or of desire; now by an act of sacrifice or thanksgiving, and in all the manners which our mind can devise.

Be not discouraged by the repugnance which you may find to it from nature; you must do yourself violence. Often, at the onset, one thinks it is lost time; but you must go on, and resolve to persevere in it till death, notwithstanding all the difficulties that may occur.

An Oratory of the Heart

Brother Lawrence wrote:

He lays no great burden upon us: a little remembrance of him from time to time; a little adoration; sometimes to pray for his grace, sometimes to offer him your sorrows, and sometimes to return him thanks for the benefits he has given you, and still gives you, in the midst of your troubles.

He asks you to console yourself with him the oftenest you can. Lift up your heart to him even at your meals and when you are in company; the least little remembrance will always be acceptable to him.

To be with God, there is no need to be continually in church. We may make an oratory of the heart wherein to retire from time to time to converse with him in humility, meekness and love.

Everyone is capable of familiar conversation with God, some more, some less. He knows what we can do. Let us begin then. Perhaps he is just waiting for one generous resolution on our part.

Have courage. We have but little time to live; you are near sixty-four, and I am almost eighty. Let us live and die with God. Sufferings will be sweet and pleasant to us while we are with him; and without him, the greatest pleasures will be anguish to us. May he be blessed for all. Amen.

Early Years

Brother Lawrence wrote:

Not finding my manner of life in books, although I have no difficulty about it, yet, for greater security, I shall be glad to know your thoughts concerning it.

In a conversation some days since with a person of piety, he told me that the spiritual life was a life of grace, which began with servile fear, which is increased by hope of eternal life, and which is consummated by pure love; that each of these states has its different stages, by which one arrives at last at that blessed consummation.

I have not followed all these methods. On the contrary, from I know not what instincts, I found that they discouraged me. This was the reason why, at my entrance into religion, I resolved to give myself up to God as the best satisfaction I could make for my sins, and for the love of him to renounce all besides.

For the first years I commonly employed myself during the time set apart for devotion with the thought of death, judgement, heaven, hell, and my sins. Thus I continued for some years, applying my mind carefully the rest of the day, and even in the midst of my business, to the presence of God, whom I considered always as with me, often as in me.

Supported

By

Faith Alone

Supported by Faith Alone

Brother Lawrence continued:

At length I came insensibly to do the same thing during my set time of prayer, which caused in me great delight and consolation. This practice produced in me so high an esteem for God that faith alone was capable to satisfy me on that point.

Such was my beginning, and yet I must tell you that for the first ten years I suffered much. The apprehension that I was not devoted to God as I wished to be, my past sins always present to my mind, and the great unmerited favours which God bestowed on me, were the matter and source of my sufferings.

During this time I fell often, yet as often rose again. It seemed to me that all creation, reason, and God himself were against me, and faith alone for me.

I was troubled sometimes with thoughts that to believe I had received such favours was an effect of my presumption, which pretended to be *at once* where others arrive only with difficulty; at other times that it was a wilful delusion, and that there was no salvation for me.

From Times of Disquiet
to Inward Peace

Brother Lawrence continued:

When I thought of nothing but to live all my days in these times of trouble and disquiet (which did not at all diminish the trust I had in God, and which served only to increase my faith), I found myself changed all at once; and my soul, which till that time was in trouble, felt a profound inward peace, as if it had found its centre and place of rest.

Ever since that time I walk before God in simple faith, with humility and with love, and I apply myself diligently to do nothing and think nothing which may displease him. I hope that when I have done what I can, he will do with me what he pleases.

As for what passes in me at present, I cannot express it. I have no pain nor any doubt as to my state, because I have no will but that of God, which I endeavour to carry out in all things, and to which I am so submissive that I would not take up a straw from the ground against his order, or from any other motive than purely that of love for him.

A Simple Attention to God

Brother Lawrence continued:

I have quitted all forms of devotion and set prayers but those to which my state obliges me. And I make it my only business to persevere in his holy presence, wherein I keep myself by a simple attention and an absorbing passionate regard to God, which I may call an actual presence of God; or, to speak better, a silent and secret conversation of the soul with God, which often causes in me joys and raptures inwardly, and sometimes also outwardly, so great that I am forced to use means to moderate them and to prevent their appearance to others.

In short, I am assured beyond all doubt that my soul has been with God above these thirty years. I pass over many things that I may not be tedious to you, yet I think it proper to inform you after what manner I consider myself before God, whom I behold as my King.

A King of Mercy and Goodness

Brother Lawrence continued:

I consider myself as the most wretched of men, full of sores and corruption, and who has committed all sorts of crimes against his King; touched with a sensible regret I confess to him all my wickedness, I ask his forgiveness, I abandon myself in his hands, that he may do what he pleases with me.

This King, full of mercy and goodness, very far from chastising me, embraces me with love, makes me eat at his table, serves me with his own hands, gives me the key of his treasures.

He converses and delights himself with me incessantly, in a thousand and a thousand ways, and treats me in all respects as his favourite.

It is thus I consider myself from time to time in his holy presence.

My most usual method is this simple attention, and such a general passionate regard to God, to whom I find myself often attached with greater sweetness and delight than that of an infant at the mother's breast: so that if I dare use the expression, I should choose to call this state 'the breasts of God', for the inexpressible sweetness which I taste and experience there.

A Stone Before a Carver

Brother Lawrence continued:

If sometimes my thoughts wander from it by necessity or infirmity, I am soon recalled by inward emotions so charming and delightful that I am confused to mention them. I beg you to reflect rather upon my great wretchedness, of which you are fully informed, than upon the great favours which God does me, all unworthy and ungrateful as I am.

As for my set hours of prayer, they are only a continuation of the same exercise. Sometimes I consider myself there as a stone before a carver, whereof he is to make a statue; presenting myself thus before God, I desire him to form his perfect image in my soul, and make me entirely like himself.

At other times, when I apply myself to prayer, I feel all my spirit and all my soul lift itself up without any trouble or effort of mine, and it remains as it were in elevation, fixed firm in God as in its centre and its resting-place.

A Holy Inactivity

Brother Lawrence continued:

I know that some charge this state with inactivity, delusion and self-love. I confess that it is a holy inactivity, and would be a happy self-love were the soul in that state capable of such; because, in fact while the soul is in this repose, it cannot be troubled by such acts as it was formerly accustomed to, and which were then its support, but which would now rather injure than assist it.

Yet I cannot bear that this should be called delusion, because the soul which thus enjoys God desires herein nothing but him. If this be delusion in me, it belongs to God to remedy it. May he do with me what he pleases; I desire only him, and to be wholly devoted to him. You will, however, oblige me in sending me your opinion, to which I always pay a great deference, for I have a singular esteem for your Reverence. . .

The Treasure of which the Gospel Speaks

Brother Lawrence wrote:

My prayers, of little worth though they be, will not fail you; I have promised it and I will keep my word. How happy we might be, if only we could find the treasure, of which the gospel tells us – all else would seem to us nothing.

How infinite it is! The more one toils and searches in it, the greater are the riches that one finds. Let us toil therefore unceasingly in this search, and let us not grow weary and leave off, till we have found. . .

I know not what I shall become: it seems to me that peace of soul and repose of spirit descend on me, even in sleep.

I only know that God keeps me; I am in a calm so great that I fear nought. What can I fear, when I am with him? And with him, in his presence, I hold myself the most I can.

May all things praise him. Amen.

Waiting Upon God in Adversity

Brother Lawrence wrote:

We have a God who is infinitely gracious and knows all our wants. I always thought that he would reduce you to extremity. He will come in his own time, and when you least expect it.

Hope in him more than ever; thank him with me for the favours he does you, particularly for the fortitude and patience which he gives you in your afflictions. It is a plain mark of the care he takes of you. Comfort yourself, then, with him, and give thanks for all.

I admire also the fortitude and bravery of M—. God has given him a good disposition and a good will, but there is in him still a little of the world and a great deal of youth. I hope the affliction which God has sent him will prove a wholesome medicine to him, and make him take stock of himself.

Let him think of God as often as he can. A little lifting up of the heart suffices. A little remembrance of God, one act of inward worship . . . are very acceptable to God.

Let him accustom himself by degrees to this small but holy exercise. No one will notice it, and nothing is easier than to repeat often in the day these little acts of inward worship.

Concerning Wandering Thoughts

Brother Lawrence wrote:

You tell me nothing new; you are not the only one that is troubled by wandering thoughts. Our mind is extremely roving; but, as the will is mistress of all our faculties, she must recall them, and carry them to God as their last end.

I believe one remedy for this is to confess our faults and to humble ourselves before God. I do not advise you to use multiplicity of words in prayer: many words and long discourses being often the occasion of wandering. Hold yourself in prayer before God like a poor, dumb, paralytic beggar at a rich man's gate. Let it be your business to keep your mind in the presence of the Lord. If it sometimes wanders and withdraws itself from him, do not much disquiet yourself for that: trouble and disquiet serve rather to distract the mind than to recall it; the will must bring it back in tranquillity.

One way to recall the mind easily in the time of prayer and to preserve it in tranquillity, is not to let it wander too far at other times. You should keep it strictly in the presence of God; and being accustomed to think of him often, you will find it easy to keep your mind calm in the time of prayer, or at least to recall it from its wanderings.

Knowing God Before Loving Him

Brother Lawrence wrote:

Our good Sister — seems to me full of goodwill, but she wants to go faster than grace. One does not become holy all at once. I commend her to you.

I am filled with shame and confusion when I reflect, on the one hand, upon the great favours which God has bestowed and is still bestowing upon me; and, on the other, upon the ill use I have made of them, and my small advancement in the way of perfection.

We cannot escape the dangers which abound in life without the actual and continual help of God. Let us, then, pray to him for it continually. How can we pray to him without being with him? How can we be with him but in thinking of him often? And how can we often think of him unless by a holy habit of thought which we should form?

You will tell me that I am always saying the same thing. It is true, for this is the best and easiest method I know; and as I use no other, I advise all the world to do it.

We must know before we can love. In order to know God, we must often think of him; and when we come to love him we shall then also think of him often, for our heart will be with our treasure.

On the Loss of a Friend

Brother Lawrence wrote:

I am very well pleased with the trust which you have in God; I wish that he may increase it in you more and more.

If M— knows how to profit by the loss he has had, and puts all his confidence in God, he will soon give him another friend, more powerful and more inclined to serve him. He disposes our hearts as he pleases. Perhaps M— was too much attached to him he has lost. We ought to love our friends, but without encroaching on our chief love which is due to God.

Remember, I pray you, what I have often recommended, which is to think often on God, by day, by night, in your business, and even in your diversions. He is always near you and with you, leave him not alone.

You would think it rude to leave a friend alone who came to visit you; why, then, must God be neglected? Do not, then, forget him, but think of him often, adore him continually, live and die with him; this is the glorious employment of a Christian. In a word, this is our profession; if we do not know it, we must learn it. I will endeavour to help you with my prayers. . .

To One Suffering Deeply

Brother Lawrence wrote:

I do not pray that you may be delivered from your troubles, but I pray God earnestly that he would give you strength and patience to bear them as long as he pleases.

Comfort yourself with him who holds you fastened to the cross. He will loose you when he thinks fit. Happy those who suffer with him.

Accustom yourself to suffer in that manner, and seek from him the strength to endure as much and as long as he shall judge to be necessary for you.

The men of the world do not comprehend these truths, nor is it to be wondered at, since they suffer as lovers of the world, and not as lovers of Christ. They consider sickness as a pain of nature, and not as from God: and seeing it only in that light, they find nothing in it but grief and distress.

But those who consider sickness as coming from the hand of God, as the effect of his mercy, and the means which he employs for their salvation – such commonly find in it great consolation.

He
Reserves
Your Cure
To Himself

He Reserves Your Cure to Himself

Brother Lawrence continued:

I wish you could convince yourself that God is often nearer to us, and more effectually present with us, in sickness than in health. Rely upon no other physician; for, according to my apprehension, he reserves your cure to himself.

Put, then, all your trust in him, and you will soon find the effects of it in your recovery, which we often retard by putting greater confidence in medicine than in God.

Whatever remedies you make use of, they will succeed only so far as he permits. When pains come from God, he alone can cure them. He often sends diseases of the body to cure those of the soul. Comfort yourself with the sovereign physician both of the soul and body.

I foresee that you will tell me that I am very much at my ease, that I eat and drink at the table of the Lord. You are right . . . but I can assure you that whatever pleasures I taste at the table of my King, my sins ever present before my eyes, as well as the uncertainty of my pardon, torment me: though in truth, that suffering itself is pleasing.

The Assurance of Faith

Brother Lawrence continued:

Be satisfied with the state in which God places you: however happy you may think me, I envy you. Pains and sufferings would be a paradise to me while I should suffer with my God, and the greatest pleasures would be a hell to me if I could relish them without him. All my joy would be to suffer something for his sake.

I must, in a little time, go to God. . . What comforts me in this life is that I now see him by faith: and I see him in such a manner as might make me say sometimes, 'I believe no more, but I see.' I feel what faith teaches us, and in that assurance and that practice of faith I will live and die with him.

Continue, then, always with God: it is the only support and comfort for your affliction. I shall beseech him to be with you. I commend myself to your prayers.

The All for the All

Brother Lawrence wrote:

Since you desire so earnestly that I should communicate to you the method by which I arrived at that habitual sense of God's presence, which our Lord, of his mercy, has been pleased to vouchsafe me, I must tell you that it is with great difficulty that I am prevailed on by your importunities; and now I do it only upon the terms that you show my letter to no one. If I knew that you would let it be seen, all the desire that I have for your perfection would not enable me to do it.

Having found in many books different methods of going to God, and divers practices of the spiritual life, I thought this would serve rather to puzzle me than facilitate what I sought after, which was nothing else than how to become wholly God's.

This made me resolve to give the all for the All; so after having given myself wholly to God, to make all the satisfaction I could for my sins, I renounced, for the love of him, everything that was not his, and I began to live as if there were none but he and I in the world.

No Small Trouble

Brother Lawrence continued:

Sometimes I considered myself before him as a poor criminal at the feet of his judge; at other times I beheld him in my heart as my Father, as my God.

I worshipped him the oftenest that I could, keeping my mind in his holy presence, and recalling it as often as I found it wandering from him. I found no small trouble in this exercise, and yet I continued it, notwithstanding all the difficulties that I encountered, without troubling or disquieting myself when my mind had wandered involuntarily.

I made this my business as much all the day long as well as at the appointed times of prayer; for at all times, every hour, every minute, even in the height of my business, I drove away from my mind everything that was capable of interrupting my thought of God.

A Holy Freedom

Brother Lawrence continued:

Such has been my common practice ever since I entered the monastic life; and though I have done it very imperfectly, yet I have found great advantages by it.

These, I well know, are to be imputed solely to the mercy and goodness of God, because we can do nothing without him, and I still less than any.

But when we are faithful to keep ourselves in his holy presence, and set him always before us, this not only hinders our offending him and doing anything that may displease him, at least wilfully, but it also begets in us a holy freedom, and, if I may so speak, a familiarity with God, wherewith we ask for, and that successfully, the graces we stand in need of.

In short, by often repeating these acts they become habitual, and the presence of God is rendered, as it were, natural to us.

Give him thanks, if you please, with me, for his great goodness towards me, which I can never sufficiently marvel at, for the many favours he has done to so miserable a sinner as I am. May all things praise him. Amen.

A Recollected State Assists Bodily Health

Brother Lawrence wrote:

If we were well accustomed to the exercise of the presence of God, all bodily diseases would be much alleviated thereby. God often permits that we should suffer a little to purify our souls and oblige us to continue with him.

I cannot understand how a soul, which is with God and which desires him alone, can feel distressed. I have had enough experience to banish all doubt on this point.

Take courage; offer him your pains unceasingly; pray to him for strength to endure them. Above all, acquire a habit of conversing often with God, and forget him the least you can.

Adore him in your infirmities, offer yourself to him from time to time, and in the very height of your suffering beseech him humbly and affectionately (as a child his good father) to grant you the aid of his grace and to make you conformable to his holy will. I shall endeavour to help you with my poor halting prayers.

Faith, Our Support in Darkness

Brother Lawrence continued:

God has many ways of drawing us to himself. He sometimes hides himself from us; but faith alone, which will not fail us in time of need, ought to be our support, and the foundation of our confidence, which must be all in God.

I know not how God will dispose of me. Happiness grows upon me. The whole world suffers; yet I, who deserve the severest discipline, feel joys so continual and so great that I can scarce contain them.

I would willingly ask of God a share of your sufferings, but that I know my weakness, which is so great that if he left me one moment to myself I should be the most wretched man alive. And yet I know not how he can leave me alone, because faith gives me as strong a conviction as sense can do that he never forsakes us until we have first forsaken him.

Let us fear to leave him. Let us be always with him. Let us live and die in his presence. Do you pray for me as I for you.

Abandonment into God's Hands

Brother Lawrence wrote:

I am in pain to see you suffer so long. What gives me some ease and sweetens the sorrow I have for your griefs is that I am convinced that they are tokens of God's love for you. Look at them in this light and you will bear them more easily.

As your case is, it is my opinion that you should leave off human remedies, and resign yourself entirely to the providence of God. Perhaps he stays only for that resignation and a perfect trust in him to cure you.

Since, notwithstanding all your cares, medicine has hitherto proved unsuccessful, and your malady still increases, it will not be tempting God to abandon yourself into his hands and expect all from him.

Love Sweetens Pain

Brother Lawrence continued:

I told you in my last letter that God sometimes permits the body to suffer to cure the sickness of the soul. Have courage, then: make a virtue of necessity. Ask of God, not deliverance from the body's pains, but strength to bear resolutely, for the love of him, all that he should please, and as long as he shall desire.

Such prayers, indeed, are a little hard to nature, but most acceptable to God, and sweet to those that love him. Love sweetens pain; and when one loves God, one suffers for his sake with joy and courage.

Do you so, I beseech you; comfort yourself with him who is the only physician of all our ills. He is the father of the afflicted, always ready to help us.

He loves us infinitely, more than we can imagine. Love him, then, and seek no other relief than in him. I hope you will soon receive it. Adieu, I will help you with my prayers, poor as they are. . .

Our Heart a Spiritual Temple

Brother Lawrence wrote:

I render thanks to our Lord for having relieved you a little according to your desire. I have been often near expiring, but I never was so much satisfied as then. Accordingly, I did not pray for any relief, but I prayed for strength to suffer with courage, humility and love.

Ah, how sweet it is to suffer with God! However great the sufferings may be, receive them with love. It is paradise to suffer and be with him; so that if even now in this life we would enjoy the peace of paradise, we must accustom ourselves to a familiar, humble, affectionate conversation with him.

We must prevent our spirit's wandering from him on any occasion. We must make our heart a spiritual temple, wherein to adore him unceasingly. We must watch continually over ourselves, that we may not do or say or think anything that may displease him. When our minds are thus filled with God, suffering will become full of sweetness, and of quiet joy.

I know that to arrive at this state the beginning is very difficult, for we must act purely in faith. But though it is difficult, we know also that we can do all things with the grace of God.

The Sweet and the Bitter

Brother Lawrence wrote:

God knows best what is needful for us, and all that he does is for our good. If we know how much he loves us, we should always be ready to receive equally and with indifference from his hand the sweet and the bitter. All would please that came from him.

The sorest afflictions never appear intolerable, except when we see them in the wrong light. When we see them as dispensed by the hand of God, when we know that it is our loving Father who abases and distresses us, our sufferings lose all their bitterness and our mourning becomes all joy.

Let our business be to know God; the more one knows him, the more one desires to know him. And as knowledge is commonly the measure of love, the deeper and more extensive our knowledge shall be, the greater will be our love; and if our love of God be great, we shall love him equally in grief and in joy.

I Hope to See Him Shortly

Brother Lawrence continued:

Let us not content ourselves with loving God for the more sensible favours, however elevated, which he has done or may do us.

Such favours, though never so great, cannot bring us so near to him as faith does in one simple act. Let us seek him often by faith. He is within us; seek him not elsewhere.

If we leave him alone, are we not rude, and do we not deserve blame, if we busy ourselves about trifles which do not please and perhaps offend him? It is to be feared these trifles will one day cost us dear.

Let us begin to be devoted to him in good earnest. Let us cast everything besides out of our hearts. He would possess them alone. Beg this favour of him. If we do what we can on our part, we shall soon see that change wrought in us which we aspire after.

I cannot thank him sufficiently for the relief he has vouchsafed you. I hope from his mercy the favour of seeing him in a few days.*

Let us pray for one another.

---

* Brother Lawrence took to his bed two days later and died within the week.

Sources and Index

The following books have been consulted:

Moeurs et Entretiens du Frère Laurent 1694, L'Abbé de Beaufort; (British Library No. 1224 616).

La Pratique de la présence de Dieu. Nouvelle édition avec préface et notes de Louis van den Bossche. Desclée de Brouwer et Cie, Paris 1934.

L'Expérience de la présence de Dieu par le Frère Laurent de la Résurrection, S. M. Boucheraux et Le R. P. François de Sainte-Marie. Editions de Seuil, Paris 1948. (British Library No. X108/8404).

The Practice of the Presence of God, translated by D. Attwater. Burns and Oates 1977. (Originally published in the Orchard series 1926).

The Spiritual Maxims of Brother Lawrence together with The Character and Gathered Thoughts. H. R. Allenson Ltd.

A Dictionary of Christian Spirituality, edited by Gordon S. Wakefield. SCM Press 1983.

The Oxford Dictionary of the Christian Church, edited by F. L. Cross. OUP 1957.

There is a small variation in dates in the works consulted. The dates of Brother Lawrence's death, conversations and letters (where dated) are, however, invariable in all accounts.

The text is that of an English translation made in 1824 and includes almost the whole of the original conversations and letters. The recurring use of the word 'that' has been omitted from the conversations as being somewhat tedious in the style presented. A few significant changes have been made after reference to the French; the English translation of 1824 was clearly slanted in some places to render it more acceptable to non-Catholic readers. There are, too, a few other amendments to effect a closer correspondence with the original.

I am gratefully indebted to all the books mentioned.

Pages	Conversation or letter number	Date	Manner of Address
23-26	C1	3 August 1666	
27-34	C2	28 September 1666	
35-41	C3	22 November 1666	
42-47	C4	25 November 1667	

48-52 (These pages record conversations based on *L'Eloge du Frere Laurent*, excepting the first paragraph on page 52 which is taken from *Moeurs et Entretiens*, both by the Abbe de Beaufort, published in 1692 and 1694 respectively.)

53-56	L1	1 June 1682 (from Paris)	Ma Révérende Mère
57-58	L2	Undated	Ma Révérende et très honorée Mère
59-60	L3	3 November 1685	Ma Révérende et très honorée Mère
61	L4	Undated	Madame (To a woman in the world)
62-70	L5	Undated	Mon Révérend Père
71	L6	Undated	Ma Révérende et très honorée Mère
72	L7	12 October 1688	Madame (To a woman in the world)
73	L8	Undated	Ma Révérende et très honorée Mère
74	L9	28 March 1689	(To the same)
75	L10	29 October 1689 (from Paris)	Madame (To a woman in the world)
76-80	L11	17 November 1690	Ma Révérende et très honorée Mère
81-83	L12	Undated	Ma Révérende Mère
85-86	L13	29 November 1690	Ma bonne Mère

86-87	L14	Undated	Ma bonne Mère
88	L15	22 January 1691	Ma très chère Mère
89-90	L16	6 February 1691	Ma bonne Mère

NOTES

Letter 12 above is often placed first in the series and there is a tradition that it was the first to be written. It certainly makes a fitting introduction and the manner of address suggests an early date. The Abbé de Beaufort, however, places it twelfth in his collection made two years after Brother Lawrence's death, and D. Attwater in the standard English text of today keeps it there, following throughout the order of the Abbé. The same order is kept here, thus making reference to the Attwater text easier for the reader.

It will be noted that much of Letter 1 is in the third person. It is written by Brother Lawrence, who no doubt found it less embarrassing to write of himself in this way.